Notes On The Distribution Of The Amaryllideae: And Of Certain Liliaceous, Irideous And Other Plants In Grand Canary, Cuba, Jamaica, And Venezuela

A. Worsley

In the interest of creating a more extensive selection of rare historical book reprints, we have chosen to reproduce this title even though it may possibly have occasional imperfections such as missing and blurred pages, missing text, poor pictures, markings, dark backgrounds and other reproduction issues beyond our control. Because this work is culturally important, we have made it available as a part of our commitment to protecting, preserving and promoting the world's literature. Thank you for your understanding.

NOTES

ON THE

DISTRIBUTION OF THE AMARYLLIDEAE

AND OF CERTAIN LILIACEOUS, IRIDEOUS
AND OTHER PLANTS

IN

GRAND CANARY, CUBA, JAMAICA, AND VENEZUELA

WITH AN

ENUMERATION OF SPECIES

BY

A. WORSLEY

LONDON:
WILLIAM WESLEY AND SON
28 Essex Street, Strand
1895

ABBREVIATIONS.

Reference to figures in Webb et Berthelot's "Histoire Naturelle des Iles Canaries" are simply entered as "Webb 230," or whatever plate number is referred to.

So also references to Ramon de la Sagra's "Flora Cubana" are entered as "Sagra" with plate number; and Bury's "Hexandrian Plants" are entered as "Bury"; and P. J. Redouté "Sur les Liliacées" as "Redouté."

PREFACE.

I SPENT the months of November and December, 1893, in Grand Canary; January and February, 1894, in Cuba; March in Venezuela; and most of April in Jamaica, and paid especial attention during this time to the Amarylliae, including in my work the undoubtedly indigenous species, those that have established themselves in these countries, and also those to be found in gardens only.

I believe that as far as Grand Canary and Jamaica are concerned, the list I give will be complete, and will also be found reliable for that part of Venezuela accessable from Caracas. I wish I could say the same for Cuba, but unfortunately the insurmountable difficulties the traveller meets with in this island, coupled with the prolonged drought prevailing during the months I was there, causes my list to be very much curtailed.

I also add a few plants belonging to other orders that chanced to come under my observation, but I have not attempted to deal with the flowering trees and shrubs, or with the ferns, except in a very rough way.

ORDER AMARYLLIDEAE.

[SUB-ORDER AMARYLLIAE.]

Grand Canary.

Crinum Augustum [Amabile].

This is found in almost every garden, and it is a striking example of how such plants get distributed from one garden to another, that out of the eighty Crinums enumerated in J. G. Baker's " Handbook to the Amaryllideae," this is the only species to be found in the Island.

Hymenocallis Caribaea.

Rare in gardens [type of Bury 28].

Pancratium Canariense.

Common in all districts. Indigenous, growing in dry places amid rocks.

Description.—*Leaves*—4 to 12, glaucous, slightly curled, channelled, distichous, persistent, up to 2 ft. long by about an inch wide.

Peduncle—up to 3 feet high, two-edged, sub-spiral.

Flowers—up to 21 to the umbel, generally fully a dozen.

Pedicels—erect, 2" to above 3" long, with a bract to each pedicel.

Seeds—freely produced, irregularly four-sided, white inside but coated jet-black, about 30 to the pod.

Fruit—green, obscurely three-valved.

Filaments—incurved.

Anthers—touching.

Narcissus Tazetta.

There are two varieties of the double-flowered form, which are both common. Indigenous.

Narcissus Broussonetii.

I found a single specimen of a very elegant form in a wild cañon near Monte. Description: about thirteen flowers to the umbel; drooping; pure white; over 1" span; cup short; tube straight, 1" long: pedicels 1½". Flowering in December.

Amaryllis Belladonna.

Not in flower during my visit, but what are undoubtedly the bulbs of this genus are common in every garden, and also in a wild state in a few places. Perhaps indigenous, but doubtfully so.

SUB-ORDER AGAVEAE.

Furcrae Elegans (var.).

Regular copses of this are found, above the cultivated zone, on the mountains between Monte and Terror. Leaves armed, 9" broad in the widest part, back smooth, sub-channelled, in an erect rosette.

Peduncle 15 ft. to 30 ft. high, flowers greenish white with a faint, unpleasant smell. Though not far removed from the Botanical Magazine plate of F. Selloa in the flowers, all these wild forms were acaulescent. In gardens I found some with distinct stems, but none of these were in flower. This fits in very well with the description of F. Elegans in J. G. Baker's "Amaryllideae," except in the one particular of the smooth-backed leaves. In all other respects the identification is complete. My description being taken from the most robust specimens, one would naturally expect the leaves, &c., to be wider than in the cultivated forms at Palermo, from which Prof. Todaro sent his description to Kew.

Agave Americana.
Common in a wild state.

Doryanthes.
Sp. in gardens.

Cuba.

[AMARYLLIAE.]

Crinum Americanum (variety).
Lagoon of San Mateo near Pinar del Rio. Indigenous. I could not obtain the flower, but have little doubt as to the species.

Hippeastrum Alberti.
Common in almost every Cuban garden, flowering in winter. H. Alberti is undoubtedly a double form of H. Equestre, and has no near affinity with H. Reginae. I may notice that I never saw a single specimen of the latter (even in gardens) in any part of Cuba, whereas the various forms of H. Equestre are to be seen everywhere.

Hippeastrum Equestre.
Several varieties. In gardens.

Hymenocallis Sp.
Probably Caribaea, unflowered. A few specimens near gardens in the S.E. districts.

Eucharis Grandiflora.
In many gardens.

Zephyranthes (two species).
Probably Z. Carinata and Z. Tubispatha or Z. Rosea, unflowered. In gardens. I searched diligently in all parts of the island without finding a sign of any of this genus in a wild state; but the prolonged drought had destroyed the last trace of all delicate herbage.

AGAVEAE.

Agave Morrisii.
Common in the S.E. districts, especially about Santiago; flowers in the winter.

Furcrae Sp.
Not the Cubensis of our gardens, unflowered. Not uncommon in S.E. districts.

Venezuela.

[AMARYLLIAE.]

Crinum Sp.
Probably C. Americanum, unflowered. Common in ditches near Caracas, between arable fields.

Crinum Sp.
A narrow, acuminate, weak-leaved, spreading, dwarf form, unflowered. Common in gardens. Perhaps "C. Graciliflorum" of Kunth.

Crinum Augustum [Amabile].
In Caracas gardens.

Hippeastrum Solandriflorum.
In dry mountain pastures between Caracas and Puerto Capello, but not common. Almost deciduous in these places. Indigenous.

Hippeastrum Equestre.
Common in gardens, and by the levadas, flowering in March; and common in a wild state in pastures, flowering with the spring rains (April or May). Indigenous. These Venezuelan forms are markedly bearded with stigma distinctly three-lobed.

Hymenocallis Moritziana, and varieties of.
Common near the coast, W. of La Guayra, but not to be found wild in the immediate vicinity of Caracas. There are many forms to be found in, or near, gardens about the capital and the suburb of Antimano, which vary in the leaf, but are similar in the flowers. Some writers make several species of them, but they have no real specific differences. These Venezuelan Hymenocallis are distinguished by a stiff, erect, large, eucharis-shaped leaf, on a long, generally winged, petiole. The flowers have very long tubes, and are generally somewhat lax. I think the forms classed as H. Undulata (not of gardens), including Borski's form, H. Moritziana, and H. Eucharidifolia, are not specifically distinct from each other. Indigenous.

Hymenocallis Caribaea.
Common in gardens. Indigenous.

Eucharis Grandiflora.
In gardens only.

AGAVEAE.

Agave Morrisii, variety.
A few specimens in the mountains. The coloration of the flowers was a bright canary yellow instead of golden as in the type.

Furcrae Sp.
Unascertained. In the mountains and hills surrounding the capital.

Jamaica.

[AMARYLLIAE.]

Crinum Jamesense (?) [C. Erubescens (?) var.]

Unflowered. This seems to be unrecorded in British works, at any rate under this name. It is of very local distribution, being a sub-aquatic, and found only on the edge of the marshes and lagoons about Palmetto Point (half-way between Arnotto Bay and Buff Bay on the N.E. coast). It was shown me by Mr. Campbell of the Castleton Botanic Gardens, who assured me that it was quite distinct from either Erubescens or Americanum. It is certainly not C. Longiflorum of Grisebach and it does not correspond with Mr. Baker's description of C. Caribaeum [C. Floridanum in part of Grisebach] in all particulars. The leaves are broader than in C. Commelyni of Jacquin. The bulbs are rather small (up to 5" dia.), cone shaped; stoloniferous; tunics rough and broken; there is no distinct basal disc, and the emission of roots from the stock occurs irregularly; leaves few, erect, short, and very blunt; the edges scabrous. Growing within a few feet of the sea, on a promontory exposed to the N.E. trade winds, and being of sub-aquatic habits, one would infer that this is an imported species. The fact of its being stoloniferous would seem to point to an American habitat. I have some bulbs under cultivation, so it will soon be possible to decide with what species this should be included. I should not be surprised if it turned out to be a white flowered form of Erubescens.

Crinum Scabrum, and vars.

Common in Jamaican Gardens. This is the very beautiful form figured in "Les Flores des Serres" [L. Van Houtte] as of Brazilian origin. Though reproducing itself freely from offsets, it does not seem to have the power of reproduction by seed in Jamaica, that is, I could find no specimen of this Crinum except where it had obviously been planted at some time. In the surroundings of old houses, uninhabited for a century, large clumps are often to be seen, and the colored men set a particular medicinal value on the juice from the bulbs.

In the Castleton Gardens I found a form like that in Bury 32, but with only 4 sessile flowers.

Crinum Giganteum.

Rare in Gardens.

Hippeastrum Reginae, and vars.

In Gardens only. I saw several fine garden forms of Reginae, such as Empress of India, etc., in the garden of Mr. Palache, near Mandeville.

Hippeastrum Equestre.

Common all over the island. Indigenous. Some scapes bore 4 flowers.

Hippeastrum Hybrids.

In Mr. Palache's beautiful garden I saw the most luxuriant specimens of H. Carnarvonia [A. D.C. Pl. Rar. Hort. Geneva 9], and others close to the old H. Johnsoni [Bury 1], and also an interesting hybrid of Solandriflora. In fact I have never seen the forms of Hippeastrum better cultivated or in more robust health than here.

Hymenocallis Speciosa.

Common in the woods and road-sides about Mandeville. The leaf varieties are endless. Indigenous.

Hymenocallis Macrostephana.

A single fine specimen in Mr. Palache's garden.

Eucharis Grandiflora.

In Gardens.

Zephyranthes Carinata.

In Gardens. I was informed at Mandeville that both this and Z. Tubispatha grew wild in the higher mountains in this part of the island.

Zephyranthes Tubispatha.

In Gardens.

[AGAVEAE.]

Furcrae Sp.

In Mountains. Unflowered, perhaps F. Cubensis.

Puerto Rico.

Hymenocallis Sp.

Probably H. Caribaea, Unflowered. A few specimens on the sandy shores between the bay of San Juan and the neighboring lagoons and marshes.

LILIACEAE.

Grand Canary.

Asphodelus Ramosus.

Very common. Flowering with the new year. Indigenous.

Asphodelus Fistulosus.

Rare. A few specimens by the sides of the lavada on the road to San Mateo. Indigenous.

Description. *Leaves*—rush like.

Stems—branched.

Bracts—short and narrow.

Flowers—small, solitary, ephemeral, resembling a minute, wide-petalled form of A. Ramosum.

Stamens—irregular in length.

Style—three-headed.

Hyacinthus Viridis, var.

Uncommon; on the N. sides of the hills between Monte and San Mateo. Indigenous. This form has two to three leaves, broader segments than the type, and a faint stink.

Yucca Sp.

Common, especially on the sides of the Telde road, just outside the Capital. This is an acaulescent, dwarf, yellow-flowered form. Flowering stems often branched.

Nothoscordum Fragrans.

Common. Indigenous.

Nothoscordum Inodorum.

Common. Indigenous.

Nothoscordum [Allium ?] Sp.

Common, and very like the preceding species in appearance, but smaller, with somewhat longer pedicels, and a very "leeky" smell. Indigenous (?).

Dasylirion Sp.

Looks like D. Glaucophyllum. Unflowered. A single specimen in the garden of Quiney's Hotel, Las Palmas.

Scilla Haemorrhoidalis (Indigenous) [Webb 230].

An interesting species, growing in deeply-shady, damp places on the northern base of a precipitous cliff about 1½ miles N.W. of Monte. [This cliff is the S. boundary of the long, wide valley running E. and W., parallel to, and about 1 mile N. of, the main road from Monte to San Mateo.] This species is dwarf, with many small purple flowers, and resembles in some ways on a minute scale those types of the genus represented in our gardens by S. Kraussii and S. Natalense.

It has also been found in the precipitous and almost uninhabited island of Hierro, but appears to affect a very limited territorial area.

Description. Slender, 12" high.

Leaves—few, shining, lanceolate, more than 12" long and greater than 1" wide as a maximum.

Stem—simple, erect, stiff, and very wiry.

Flowers—numerous, borne singly on a long loose spike. They are very small [less than ¼ of a inch dia.], heliotrope coloured with a purple germen, and scentless. About 3 are open at once.

Fruit—as large as the flowers, forming within about two days.

Lilium Longiflorum. [Indigenous?]

In gardens, but not common. It thrives most luxuriantly, however, when any care is taken.

Cuba.

Aloe Vera.

Not uncommon.

Venezuela.

Lilium Longiflorum.
Common in gardens.

Jamaica.

Hemerocallis Fulva.
In gardens about Mandeville.

Agapanthus Umbellatus.
In gardens, but not common.

IRIDEAE.

Grand Canary.

Antholiza Aethiopica.
Common about Monte, both in gardens and in the wild rocky barancas, but I never found it very far from houses or gardens. Flowers about Christmas, and is very true to the type of Redouté.

It grows with a branched stem about five feet high, bearing up to 74 flowers to the spike. The flowers are reddish-yellow, the upper segment red, but when immature there is much green about them.

Gladiolus Sp.—Indigenous (?).
Near G. Segetum. In arable land near Santa Brigida, growing amongst the maize. Flowers in December.

Description. *Stems*—slender, waved, often branched, about two feet high.

Flowers—about a dozen, borne singly on a loose spike, bright amathystine purple.

Segments—the upper much the largest, 2" long by ¾" wide, the wing segments shorter with a deeper purple keel in most cases. The 3 lower segments marked with a claw and white keel. The base of all the segments (except the upper) being marked with a cross line of dark colour, forming an irregular ring round the lower part of the throat.

Spathes—large, erect.

Ixia (?) Sp.
In cornfields near Ginamar. Unflowered, but I have bulbs under cultivation.

Iris Florentina.
Growing wild in the barancas about Monte. This form has a faint but very sweet odor, which I have noticed, under certain conditions, in English gardens.

Iris Florentina (?), variety.
This is a purple form found in the same localities as the type. It is odorless, more than one flower to the stem, and much taller, but otherwise like Iris Pumilum Violaceum of Redouté 261. Standards bifurcate.

Venezuela.

Iris Japonica (?).

What is apparently a small form of I. Jap. Fimbriata [Chinensis], in gardens only. March.

Sisyrinchium Sp.

A yellow form. In mountains N.W. of Caracas. Common in this locality: flowering in March.

Trimezia Meridensis.

Common in mountains N.W. of Caracas, especially near the coast. This may grow in Merida province also, but not exclusively there. Flowers in March.

Alophia Liniaris.

Western provinces. Personally I was unable to gather this in flower.

Gladiolus Sp.

Unascertained. This is a tall, semi-patent form; flowers blood-red spotted with yellow. In gardens only, flowering in March.

This is the only species of Gladiolus I could find in the Caracas neighbourhood, and it was fairly common.

Cuba.

I saw no irideous plants whatever in the island.

Jamaica.

Trimezia Martinensis.

Common about Castleton, growing in damp pastures.

Gladiolus Sp.

In gardens. This is the same form that I found about Caracas. In the Mandeville district it flowers about April. I could find no other Gladiolus species in Jamaican gardens.

ORCHIDEAE.

Grand Canary.

Habenaria Tridactylites (of Lindley). [Webb. 221.]

Not uncommon in damp places on rocky hills about Monte. Flowers inconspicuous, greenish, slightly fragrant. Scape naked, 6^v to $12^\wedge$ high bearing about 15 flowers, spathes clinging. Leaves, two.

Cuba.

——— (genus doubtful.)

Unascertained. An Epiphytic orchid, growing in deep shade in the woods about the Penupo Manganese mines. Unfortunately, I lost all my specimens through an accident in crossing the river on my return journey. Description—Flowers, dark purple and green, small, fragrant, produced successively on a long, loose simple scape. Root-stock small, leaf-stem a yard or more in length, bearing about a dozen stiff large alternate evergreen leaves. Flowering in March.

Bletia Verecunda.

Growing on the N. side of very dry rocky cuttings on the roadside between Cristo and Guantanamo. Flowering in March. Indigenous. This form is quite deciduous, the flowers purple-pink.

This form does not correspond with any figure or description in Sagra's work. The inflorescence is most like his figure of B. Tenera, of which he states that it grows near Santiago de Cuba, and is an undoubtedly new species. He adds, "In parte superiore simplici aut ramoso," but I have noticed this in B. Shepherdi. Certainly in this Cuban form the raceme is not so dense, and the leaves very narrow; but the close connection that subsists between the flora of Jamaica and that of south-eastern Cuba would favor the supposition that there is no good specific difference between these two forms. However, the root stocks are dissimilar.

The plants I found fit in, from a botanical point of view, with B. Verecunda, but I have never seen a figure of this species which quite satisfies me.

Venezuela.

Epidendrum Elongatum.

Growing between the cracks in the rocks in dry, shady places on the mountains between Caracas and the coast. This species found sustenance where a few inches of sticks, moss, or fibrous rubbish had become lodged on the rock. Flowering in March. Altitude about 4500 feet. Indigenous.

Spiranthes Elata (of Lindley).

Common in damp, shady places in the same locality as the preceding. Flowering in March. Indigenous.

Cattleya Mossiae (var.)

Flowering in April. The lip is of a very rich orange-brown, and the flowers very fragrant. This was given me by a friend in Caracas. Locality unascertained. I am informed that there are not so many Cattleyas as formerly in those parts of Venezuela which are of tolerably easy access. Certainly, in the Caracas neighbourhood there are now none to be found. Indigenous.

Jamaica.

Bletia Shepherdi.

Fairly common on road-sides about Castleton. April.

Epidendrum Fragrans.

Common in woods about Castleton. April.

Spiranthes Elata (of Lindley.)

Common in damp pastures about Castleton. April. Indigenous.

Spiranthes (Stenorrynchus) Orchioides.

In dry pastures by the sides of the Wag Water, near the coast. April. This has many flesh-colored flowers, borne on a tall, stout scape, which appears before the leaf-growth has begun. The flowers have a beautifully "frosted" appearance. The roots resemble those of many species of Alstroemeria. Indigenous.

Dendrobium species.
Hope and Castleton gardens.

Phaius Grandifolius.
Not uncommon at altitudes of about 3000 feet on the Blue Mountains. Spring.

Broughtonia Sanguinea.
In shady places along the N.E. coast. April.

——————— (genus unascertained.)
A grey-purple flowered ground orchid from gardens at Mandeville. Said also to grow on the higher mountains at the western end of the island. April.

Some of the natives call this the "Resurrection Plant," others the "Jamaica Crocus." It is well worth cultivation.

Description—Roots like those of Spiranthes Orchioides. From the junction of the tubers rises an underground sheath containing a number of flowers which expand in succession immediately on pushing through the ground, thus maintaining the flowering period for some weeks. The two upper segments of the corolla are large and erect, the rest smaller and more or less lax. The general resemblance to a crocus is sufficient to account for the name given locally. Should this prove to be a little-known species, I will add a detailed description of the flowers [and leaves, which have not yet appeared]; but these specimens were only presented to me as I was *en route* to embark on the steamer on my way back to England, and I have had no time to examine them.

Oncidium Luridum.
Common in woods about Mandeville. April. Larger in all parts than any cultivated or dried specimens of this genus that I have seen.

AROIDEAE.
Grand Canary.

Arisarum Vulgare. [A Subexertum?]
Very common. December. There are at least two varieties, and many color varieties. One variety which might be called "Viridis" has a spathe the exterior green, whitish below, the interior marked with broad clear bands and veins of purple brown running vertically. There are no spots on the spathe. Another very dainty form has a spathe white below striped and dotted purple with a deep purple hood. Both forms have spotted stems and in some cases the leaves are spotted white.

Alocasia Esculenta.
Common in ditches.

Amorphophallus sp.
   Rare in gardens. Like Rivieri in leaf. Unflowered.

Arum Dracunculus.
   Common above Monte on the San Maeto road by the sides of the lavada in damp shady places. This is perhaps identical with the " Dracunculus Canariensis" of Webb, plate 219.

Cuba.

Pothos (?) sp.
   On tree trunks by the sides of the small streams and lagoons about San Mateo and Guayabo, in the Province of Pinar del Rio.

Alocasia Esculenta.
   Common.

Alocasia Species (2)
   There are two other species occasionally met with, which are distinct from A. Esculenta, but to what species they belonged I was unable to determine. One of them was a small growing form. Both are plain green in leaf.

Anthurium Acanle (var.)
   Common in woods, and growing to a large size. Not strictly acaulescent, nor possessing the fragrance of the type.

Philodendron Sp.
   A climbing and rambling plant. Very common in shady places. This is quite distinct from P. Selloum, though not far removed from it. The seedlings do not assume their true leaf-imbrication until the 5th or 6th leaf is developed.

Caladium Wightii, C. Chantini, C. Bicolor and vars.
   In gardens these were most commonly met with, though I noticed other forms as well.

Venezuela.

Anthurium Acanle (var.)
   The same species as in Cuba, but not so common.

Philodendron sp.
   Common. Same species as in Cuba.

Jamaica.

Alocasia Esculenta.
   Common.

Alocasia sp. (2).
   Same species as in Cuba. Not uncommon.

Philodendron sp.
   Same species as in Cuba. Common in woods about Castleton. This large and striking aroid cannot fail to attract the attention of the most unobservant. It seems strange that there should be any doubt as to the species.

Philodendron sp.

A smaller form with 3-lobed leaf, showing much variation in shape. Road-sides about Castleton. I did not notice this to be a climber, but mostly running along the ground, or hanging over cliffs.

Caladium sps. (3) and vars.

The same species that I noticed in Cuba also obtain in Jamaican Gardens. There are many others also.

MISCELLANEOUS.

Grand Canary.

Adiantum sp.

A very beautiful form, and perhaps some variety of A. tenerum. Stems black, shining; fronds of an almost transparent green of a very light shade.

I found this only in caves in the same locality as Scilla haemorrhoidalis. These caves are mostly at the base of a precipitous cliff facing N., and are generally full of water, the ferns depending from the roofs, their roots clinging to the soft, porous rock—there is absolutely no soil for them. The light coloration of the fronds is perhaps dependent upon the deep shade in which they grow.

Arundo Donax Variegata.

In gardens. Not to be confused with A. Versicolor.

Cineraria Sp.

Common between Monte and San Mateo. Dec. and Jan.

This is a tall growing form, with annual stems. Flowers in clusters, ¾ of an inch in diam., whitish with a mauve tinge, the disk purple.

Chrysanthenum Annuum.

Common about Ginama. Dec. Flowers generally white with a yellow center, but there are several color varieties in white and yellow.

Dianthus sp.

On road sides near Monte, but not common. Dec.

A very minute, pale pink, dwarf form, expanding single flowers in succession from a spathe terminating an erect stem.

Musa Cavendishii.

Zebra-marked "sports," common but not persistent. Gardens.

Oxalis Cernua.

Common in damp places. This luxuriates marvellously; in some pastures nothing else will grow (at any rate in winter), and this oxalis form a thick crop half-a-foot high, covered, on sunny days, with a dazzling carpet of yellow bloom. These pastures are regularly cut for fodder during the winter, and, on examining several loads, I found that quite 90 per cent. was composed of this oxalis

Whether it is good fodder or not, I am unable to say, but it should be born in mind that fodder is very expensive and generally very bad in Grand Canary. Webb, Lowe and others do not mention this Sp.

Plumbago Capensis.
In hedges on the San Mateo Road, flowering in winter.

Strelitzia Nicolai.
In gardens. This grows 12 to 15 feet high, and flowers freely in autumn.

Strelitzia Reginae.
Common in gardens, as also are many proliferous forms. Autumn and winter.

Strelitzia Reginae, var. Pumila.
This is to be found in almost every garden, being more common than the type, from which it is easily distinguished. Autumn and winter.

Sempervivum Chrysanthum (?)
What seems to be a large form of this, or of some closely allied species, is very common in all the barancas and cliffs. Flowering in winter.

Vinca Major.
Common in the Barancas about Monte, in damp situations. Winter.

Viola Madeiriensis.
Common about San Mateo. Winter.

Codiaeum sp. and vars.
Gardens. Turning all but deciduous in winter, and presenting a woeful aspect.

Euphorbia Pulcherrima.
Gardens. Common. Though growing to be small trees (I saw one at Guia 20 feet high and quite as thick), and bearing a profusion of bloom in winter, this species is quite deciduous in this climate.

Cuba.

Alpinia Nutans.
In the S.E districts, about Dos Bocas and Penupo. Spring.

Adiantum Pedatum (?)
Common in several varieties all over the island. None of the forms are quite true to the N. American type.

Adiantum Cristatum.
By the sides of streams about Pinar del Rio.

Mimosa Pudica.
Common.

Plumeria Tricolor.
　　This tree is to be found about Santiago, in gardens only, flowering in March.

Codiaeum, many species and vars.
　　In gardens. They thrive well where properly tended.

Euphorbia Pulcherrima.
　　In gardens. Jan. to Feb.

Davallia fumarioides.
　　A dwarf, armed fern, with creeping root-stock, growing in dry woodlands on the hills about Guayabo in the province of Pinar del Rio.

Pinguiculata Filifolia.
　　A delicate, white flowered, horn-shaped plant; flowers born singly on very slender scapes about 6" high. From the dried up Savannas of Pinar del Rio. Jan.

Lomaria attenuata (?)
　　On the steep and shady banks of streams in the western districts. Here the streams cut deep channels through the light, sandy soil.

Chloris Polydactyla.
　　Common.

Lindenia rivalis.
　　By the sides of streams in the woods of the S.E. districts about Dos Bocas. Half hidden in the grass, I mistook these in the distance for Zephyranthes, for which at the time I was earnestly searching. The star-shaped, pure white flowers made a very tolerable imitation.

Asclepias (several forms).
　　Common all over the island.

Jatropha Podagrica.
　　About Caney near Santiago. March. Fairly common.

Puerto Rico.

Nimosa Pudica.
　　Common.

Asclepias (vars.)
　　Common.

Venezuela.

Rhynchospora Stellata.
　　Not uncommon about Caracas.

Isoloma sp.
　　Near I. Mollis. Common in gardens at Antimano. March.

Heliconia Psittacorum.
　　I found a few specimens in flower in a gorge among the mountains of the coast range (alt. 4500 ft.). March.

Codiaeum (sps. and vars.)
  In gardens, but not florishing.

Anoda Hastata.
  About Caracas, on the dry mountain slopes above the cemetery. Flowering in March.

Chloris Polydactila.
  Common.

Gymnogramme Calomelanos.
  Common about Caracas.

Salvia sp.
  A bright red, small flowered form, by the sides of the irrigation ditches in the valley of the Guayre river above Caracas. March.

Jamaica.

Nimosa Pudica.
  Common.

Rhynchospora Stellata.
  Common about Castleton.

Alpinia Nutans and A. Erecta.
  Not uncommon; the latter in gardens only. March.

Adiantum Tenerum.
  Very fine forms of this on the N.E. coast. Near Arnotto Bay I gathered the finest specimens of this species that I have ever seen.

Heliconia Psittacorum.
  In Hope Gardens. April.

Ipomoea Quamoclit.
  I gathered this charming little annual by the side of a ditch in some uncultivated ground attached to the Hope Gardens. This was in April, but I understand that it is to be gathered wild, flowering generally after the rains begin.

Codiaeum (sps. and vars.)
  In Castleton gardens there is the best display of this genus I have ever seen, and in the most luxuriant health.

Jasminum (?) sp.
  A very elegant, yellow flowered, scentless form. April.
  I only found a single specimen, on the roadside below Gordon Town.

Oxalis sp.
  A pink form, not unlike our own. April. Common.

Musa Coccinea.
  Castleton Gardens. April.

Zingiber officinale (Ginger).
  This has escaped, and now grows wild by the sides of the Wag Water, flowering in spring.

―――― (genus unascertained.)

A large yellow flowered, umbellate, leguminosious plant, climbing in hedges. April. I found a single specimen only near Palmetto Point, on the N.E. coast.

Pitcairnia Bromeliaefolia.

This corresponds very well with Redouté's figure. Common between Castleton and Arnotta Bay, on shady cliffs. April.

Aechmea, sps. (2).

There are at least two species of large parasitic Aechmeas, one of which is armed in the lower half.

Begonia, sps. (2).

Two sub-shrubby forms, at least, are to be met with in a wild state, but neither possesses any horticultural value. April.

Chloris Polydactyla.

Common.

Gymnogramme Calomelanos.

Common, about Castleton especially.

Asclepias (2 forms).

Common in the western districts.

Winter-Flowering Plants, &c., of Cuba.

Among the wretched tangled scrub that covers so much of the island, Convolvuli (Pharbitis Sps.), in various shades of blue, purple, and white, are very common; also a few Ipomoeas in some places, and a small-flowered yellow sub-shrubby plant. There is also an infinity of flowering leguminoseae, mostly of the pea tribe, none of which appeared to me to have any horticultural value. The fences are brightened by the coral-colored, deciduous piñon, which produces its terminal racemes in February and March. The most striking object (in the latter month) in the hedges is a bromeliaceous plant, not unlike the wild pine-apple, which produces a set of most brilliant carmine-red leaf bracts.

Taken altogether, I have never been in a country so nearly flowerless in the winter-time as Cuba, and this notwithstanding the delightful weather that invariably prevails at this season. In the S.E. districts, Artocarpus Incisifolia has established itself in the woods. One character of the landscape is the profusion of epiphytal bromeliads on deciduous trees.

Winter-Flowering Plants, &c., of Grand Canary.

The Euphorbias in many forms and Opuntias cover the uncultivated parts of the Island. The candelabra-like Euphorbias show an unmistakable alliance with the flora of Africa, and give a hard and repellant aspect to the poor, stony lands of the interior. Opuntias [Nopaleas] were largely grown to support the cochineal insect, but of recent years it has been found possible to produce the most brilliant carmine dyes by another and a cheaper process, and this cochineal industry has almost perished. It still continues to be carried out in a desultory way in parts of the Island, but the vast acreage planted with these Opuntias is now of little value except as food for swine. The imprint of famine—endemic, unmistakable—is stamped upon the goats, dogs, pigs, and other animals of the island. Only this could drive either swine or goats to consume such distressful food, though of course only the young growth is chosen for them, and the spines are removed.

Agave Americana is used for fencing, and very picturesque these fences become—interspersed with tall, scraggy pelargoniums, and, in many places, with a sweet-scented white broom and Plumbago Capensis. These pelargoniums have run wild in almost every old hedge and on the sides of the rocky barancas, and, even in mid-winter, are all more or less in flower. The double forms are quite as common as the single, and seem, singularly, much more robust and floriferous. Reds and pinks are in many shades, but no white forms in a wild state.

There are two very striking and common yellow flowers blooming in mid-winter—one is Oxalis Cernua, which covers many damp pastures, and opens fully only on sunny days; the other is a sub-shrubby Sempervivum, which I take to be S. Chrysanthum, or something nearly allied to it. The white star-like flowers of Aphodelus Ramosus cover large tracts of marshy uplands, mostly on steep hill-slopes with a northern aspect, and grow surrounded by Nothoscordum Sps., and various small-growing Alliums. Antholiza Aethiopica is very conspicuous in a few places.

GARDEN NOTES.

Gardening in Grand Canary is at a very low ebb, and seems to be about the last thing the inhabitants think about. The only garden worth looking at is that of Count Phillipe Maseu, midway on the road between Las Palmas and San Mateo.

Señor Lugo has a pleasant little palm grove at the Capital, but this is all there is worth seeing in the island. In considering to what a great extent the flora of the Cape has found its way to Grand Canary, it should be borne in mind that even in these latter days of large steamships it is necessary for the major part of the shipping between Europe and the Cape to call at the Canaries for coal or provisions.

Gardening in Cuba is a thing practically unknown. The place near the house where the garden ought to be is turned into a rubbish heap in 99 cases out of 100. Even round the largest houses of the wealthiest inhabitants, a palm grove and a few flowering acacia trees is about the limit in this direction—something that wants no attention, and that no neglect can kill. It is not necessary in Cuba to discriminate between "species" and "forms of garden origin;" of the latter kind—there are not any. For a scene of utter neglect and misery go to the so-called Botanic Gardens, such as that at Matanzas.

Gardening in Venezuela is far from being so neglected. In the Capital there are many pleasant gardens carefully tended, and the Government gardens on the hill of Calvary, overlooking the city, are well worth a visit.

In Jamaica gardening is studied, and much taste is shown in the majority of cases. Castleton gardens are in some ways the most beautiful I have seen, though a great part of their charm lies in their mountain entourage, and in the exuberant vegetation with which this is clothed. Hope gardens are extensive, but in a very incomplete state at present.

A Group of Furcraeas in Grand Canary.

On November 20th, from a great distance I espied, through my glasses, something interesting. After a climb of many hours I found myself in a perfect forest of Furcraeas; fully a hundred were out in bloom at once, quite close together. They ran up from 15' to 30' in height. I have seldom seen a more beautiful sight than was presented by their graceful, fern-like plumes, clear cut against precipices of black rock, or a background of azure sky. In Grand Canary this form propagates itself from seed freely, and so of course it is possible that some of the galleons trading between the Spanish main and Cadiz brought the first seeds over to Canary. It has certainly now established itself firmly in the island.

Ferns of Cuba.

There are many species which I am not qualified to determine. I noticed a gigantic maidenhair, with black, coarse, and very tough stems (up to 5 ft. high), and a spread of fronds about a yard wide. This form is evergreen, and quite common in woods between Santiago and Cristo. About Pinar del Rio there are some forms of Adiantum Cristatum very stiff and wiry, with fronds as hard as, and shaped like, fish scales.

In the dry woods on the hills between Guayabo and Peña Blanca, I found Davallia fumarioides (of Swartz) an elegant, dwarf, armed fern, with creeping root-stock. Near Pinar del Rio, I saw a very tough, leathery kind of hart's tongue, a small form of the common British fern, and also a bracken similar to ours.

Ferns of Jamaica.

The display of ferns in the Castleton district, even in the hedgerows only, is quite unmatched by anything I have seen elsewhere. The heavy dews, the equable temperature, and the constant moisture maintained by the play of the N.E. trade winds upon these (relatively) cool highlands, has here produced a perfect paradise for ferns and mosses. I have heard it said that over 500 different species of ferns could be counted along the road-side within a mile or so of Castleton. A species of tree-fern is very noticeable, and the same giant maidenhair that I found in Cuba is also here, but does not seem to attain quite the same stature. I noticed especially the wonderful height of some of the mosses (Lycopodium

Cernuum), and of a peculiar straggling, armed bracken. Adiantum Tenerum, and something not far from A. Pedatum luxuriate. In the Mandeville district there is nothing like the same display of ferns, and although a great number grow in this district, they begin here to assume that same tough and drought-resisting aspect that characterise the ferns of Cuba.

Vine and Sugar Cultivation, Etc.

The vine florishes in Grand Canary, but the cultivation is of the rudest kind. The plants grow like small currant bushes, and beyond cutting them back once a year, and scratching a hole round the base of each vine (to allow the rain to accumulate in a pool), nothing much is done at them.

It must be noted, however, that the soil of the island is deep and of such a light scoriaceous nature that spade-culture is impracticable. The natives use a tool like a heavy large turf-cutter bent at right angles to the handle; this they raise above the head and allowing it to fall deep into the soil they draw the weapon towards them, thus scraping a hole among the cinders.

The rain falls in heavy storms, mostly in winter, and perhaps not more than four or five times in the year. The vines are grown on precipitous slopes and something must be done to catch what falls in the way of rain.

Arundo Donax is grown in every damp place. The canes are cut into lengths of about 18 inches, split, and chamfered at the end, thus forming a niche.

These split canes are used for supporting the vine branches and preventing them trailing upon the ground.

As for the product of these labors I cannot speak favourably. The red "Vino de pays" is simply villainous and has an unaccountable flavor of indiarubber about it. The white wines are strongly fortified, and, if kept long enough, are very fair as liqueur wines. They are intermediate in flavour between Madeira and Marsala. Their alcoholic strength is very high.

Neither in Cuba, Venezuela or Jamaica did I see the vine cultivated, nor could I obtain native wines made from the grape. In Havana there is quite a large industry in fabricating wines, of which clarified rum is the basis. I understand that cultivation of the vine is here prohibited in deference to the wishes of Spanish wine growers.

The sugar cane is cultivated on the littoral of Grand Canary, especially about Guia, and the natives seem to take a more intelligent interest in cane growing than in anything else. The cultivation is good, the canes robust and finer than anything I saw in Cuba, Jamaica or Venezuela. But the mills are very primitive and lack of capital is apparent on all sides.

In Cuba the Sugar Cane grows without much labor in the deep soils of the plains between Havana and Cienfuegos, and also about Guantanamo.

The cultivation is of the rudest and most reckless kind, but magnificent machinery is made use of on the larger ingenios [sugar estates] for crushing and granulating. This state of things being the exact reverse of what I found in Gran Canary.

In Venezuela the cane is grown in the valleys of the Guayre and other rivers and most carefully cultivated and irrigated. But the estates are mostly small and cannot afford the best machinery, and the soil is stony and light. Besides which, at times, these valleys are subject to disastrous "wash outs," caused, I believe, by the deforesting of the mountains, and consequent sudden rush of water following the torrential rains. These seem to recur about every fifth or sixth year.

In Jamaica the soil is (taken as a whole) so poor compared with that of Cuba that I regard cane growing as a doomed industry in this island. In Jamaica good land for sugar growing exists, but it is impossible to find a large acreage of rich soil in one locality sufficient to support undertakings of great importance, such as exist in Cuba.

In conclusion my thanks are due to my most estimable friend Prof. Ernst, of Caracas, for the assistance he gave me in obtaining plants and specimens, and in fixing the species of certain forms with which I was unacquainted; and also to Messrs. J. G. Baker, W. B. Hemsley, and R. A. Rolfe, at Kew, in kindly ascertaining the species or affinities of several Orchids, Ferns, etc., of which I brought back specimens and descriptions.

Printed by Libri Plureos GmbH in Hamburg, Germany